LAST MINUTE REVISION

GCSE
BIOLOGY
Booster

First published 2000
exclusively for WHSmith by

Hodder & Stoughton Educational
338 Euston Road
London NW1 3BH

Text and illustrations © Hodder & Stoughton Educational 2000

Illustrations on pages 8, 14 (top), 35 (top) © David Applin

All rights reserved. No part of this publication may be reproduced or transmitted in any form or by any means, electronic or mechanical, including photocopying, recording or any information storage and retrieval system, without permission in writing from the publisher.

A CIP record for this book is available from the British Library.

Text: Viv Cooper
Illustrations: Helen Humphreys
Developed and edited by Hart McLeod

ISBN 0 340 781 300

Printed and bound by Hobbs The Printer, Totton, Hants.

Acid rain

Rain is always slightly acidic. However, human activities, particularly burning fossil fuels in power stations and cars, make it very acidic.

- **Sulphur dioxide** and **nitrogen oxides** dissolve in water droplets in clouds and fall as acid rain.
- Acid rain releases **heavy metal ions** from soil, e.g. aluminium, which poison tree roots on land and fish in water. Trees and fish die. Whole lakes can die.
- Limestone buildings and statues can be worn away too.

Adaptation

The features of an organism which help it live in its environment.

Cacti live in hot, dry deserts where water is a problem.

- They have swollen stems in which they can store water.
- Their **outer stems** are **waterproof**.
- Their **leaves** are reduced to **spines** so there is **less surface area** to lose water from. These successful adaptations allow them to deal with the difficult conditions.

Polar bears have adaptations to survive in the cold, frozen desert of the Arctic.

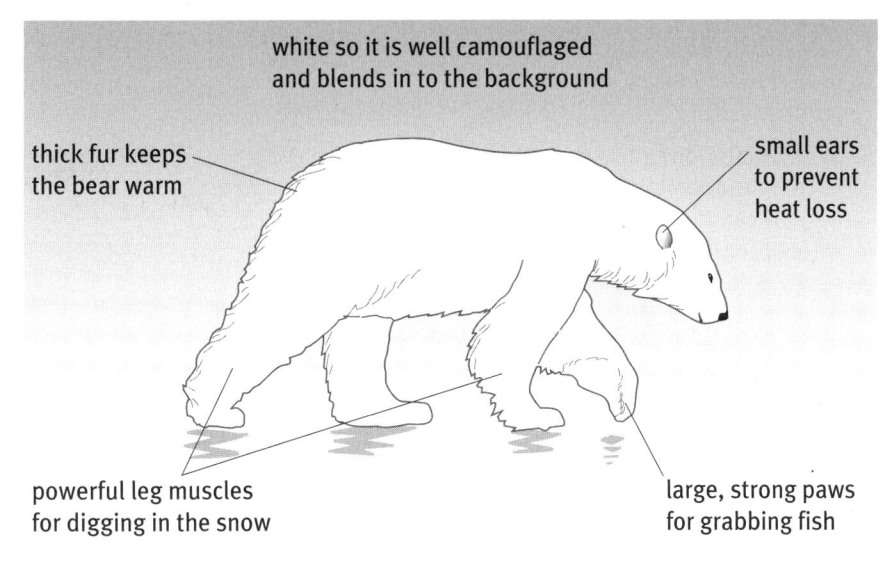

- white so it is well camouflaged and blends in to the background
- thick fur keeps the bear warm
- small ears to prevent heat loss
- powerful leg muscles for digging in the snow
- large, strong paws for grabbing fish

Alcohol

Alcohol is an ingredient of a range of drinks including beer, wine, cider and spirits like gin and whisky.

- Alcoholic drinks come in different strengths, measured as a % by volume. The higher the % the more alcohol it has. Alcopops often have a very high %. The effect depends on the strength of the drink, how fast it is consumed, whether a person has eaten, their weight, mood and the surroundings.
- It is illegal to sell alcohol to under-18s (unless 16 and having a meal in a restaurant). Police have the legal power to confiscate alcohol from under-18s.
- Alcohol is a **depressant drug**. It poisons the nervous system and affects judgement and self-control. Speech can become slurred and it reduces the power of coordination. Heavy drinking can lead to unconsciousness and coma and a risk of choking on vomit. Long-term over-use can lead to serious liver, heart and stomach problems.
- More than 25 000 deaths in the UK are alcohol-related.
- Mixing alcohol with other drugs is **seriously dangerous**.

Asexual reproduction

A type of reproduction with only one parent, producing genetically identical offspring.

- Gametes (sex cells) are not produced in asexual reproduction.
- Many plants, fungi, bacteria and some animals can reproduce without sex.
- Each new individual receives an **exact copy** of the parent's genetic material by mitosis and can be called a **clone**.

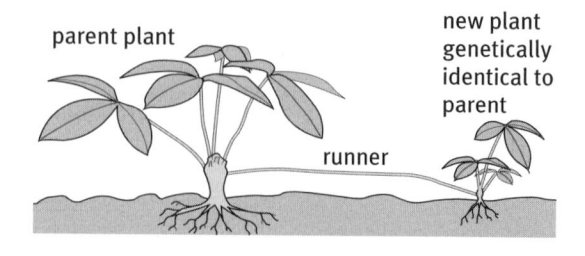

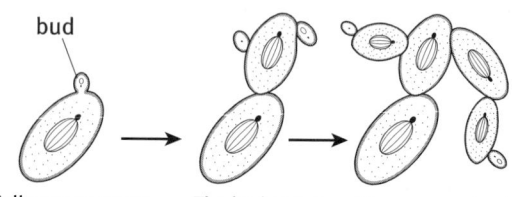

parent plant

new plant genetically identical to parent

runner

bud

Fully grown yeast cell forming a bud.

The bud grows and forms more buds, making a chain of yeast cells.

Bacteria

Bacteria are single-celled microorganisms, sometimes made up of chains or clusters.
- They can only be seen under a microscope.
- They are found everywhere: in water, in the air and in the soil.
- They have a different structure inside from most living things.
- They do not have a proper nucleus.
- Their DNA is in the form of a ring.

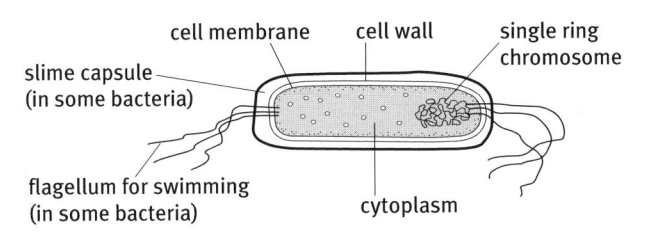

cell membrane, cell wall, single ring chromosome, slime capsule (in some bacteria), flagellum for swimming (in some bacteria), cytoplasm

- They have a variety of shapes which helps to identify them.

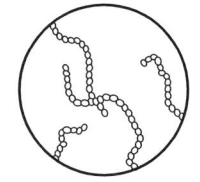

Streptococci (sore throat)   **Bacilli (tetanus)**   **Vibrio (cholera)**

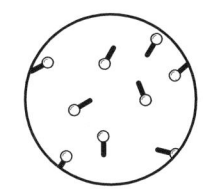

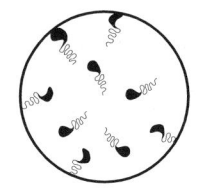

- Most bacteria are harmless. They feed by pouring enzymes onto food, e.g. a dead leaf or a piece of bread, and then absorbing the digested food. They are **saprophytes**. This causes decay which is important in nutrient recycling, but also causes human food to go off.
- Some bacteria are **parasites**. They feed on the living tissues of other organisms and cause them harm (a disease), e.g. whooping cough, tetanus and meningitis.
- Bacteria can be killed outside a body by chemicals called **antiseptics**. Drying, pickling, salting and heat treatments can also kill them. Freezing slows down their growth so helps keep food fresh.
- **Disease-causing** bacteria are **killed** in humans by **white blood cells** and our **immune systems**. **Antibiotics** can help us fight off the bacteria by killing them. Fleming was the first to discover the antibiotic properties in the mould *Penicillium*.
- Bacteria are widely used in **biotechnology** and **genetic engineering**.

Biodiversity

The vast range of living things in the world (1.7 million already described) is known as biodiversity.

Species are divided into six main groups in this chart. The most common species are in the arthropods, which includes all the insects. The great variety of living organisms are classified (put into groups) according to the features they have.

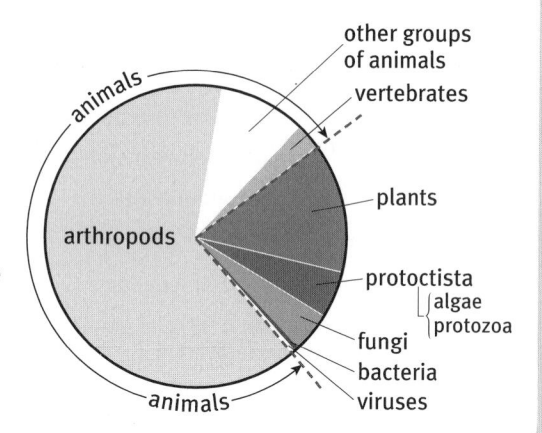

Biotechnology

Biotechnology is the way we use plant cells, animal cells and microorganisms to produce substances which are useful to us. For thousands of years we have exploited yeast to make wine, beer and bread. They depend on the process of fermentation in which:

- sugars are turned into ethanol (alcohol) by yeast
- carbon dioxide is produced as a by-product
- no air can be present, as this causes the alcohol to turn to vinegar
- Glucose + Water $\xrightarrow{yeast}$ Ethanol + Carbon dioxide.

In **wine** the glucose can come from any source, often fruit, like grapes. In beer making, the sugar comes from germinating barley grains (malt) and in **bread-making** it is the carbon dioxide that makes the dough rise.

Lactic acid bacteria have been used to make yoghurt from milk. Nowadays we use biotechnology to make:

- medicines
- enzymes for anything from washing powders to removing lactose from milk
- biofuel
- bioinsecticides
- single-cell protein, e.g. quorn and many more.

Blood

It moves substances rapidly from one part of the body to another and prevents infections entering through breaks in the skin. It contains several different components.

- **Red blood cells** contain haemoglobin which carries oxygen from the lungs to all cells in the body. They have no nucleus.

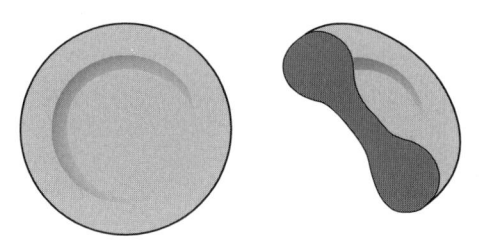

- **White blood cells** kill off invading microbes. They defend against diseases.

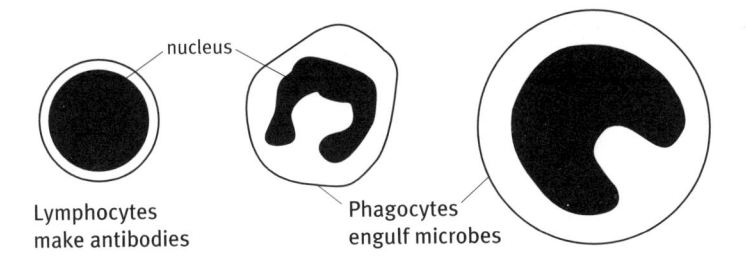

  Lymphocytes make antibodies
  Phagocytes engulf microbes

- **Platelets** are small pieces of cells. They release chemicals which cause blood to clot.

- **Plasma** is a pale yellow solution containing sugars, salts, urea, hormones, carbon dioxide and proteins such as antibodies. Heat is also distributed by the plasma.

Body systems

There are nine major organ systems in the human body.

System	Function/Job	Main organs
digestive system	breaks down food into simpler substances so they can be absorbed and used by the body	stomach and small intestine
respiratory system	takes in oxygen and removes waste carbon dioxide	windpipe, lungs, ribs and diaphragm
excretory system	removes poisonous waste materials which are made in the body	kidneys
circulatory system	transports materials around the body	heart, arteries, veins and capillaries
reproductive system	produces offspring	ovaries, oviducts, uterus in females; testes, sperm ducts, penis in males
nervous system	controls and coordinates the whole body.	brain, spinal cord, nerves
endocrine system	produces and releases chemicals called hormones from special glands.	glands, e.g. pituitary pancreas, adrenals, thyroid, testes/ovaries
skeletal system	gives support and points for muscle attachment and protects organs	206 bones of the body
muscle system	allows movement of the body	antagonistic pairs of muscles, e.g. biceps/tricep

Breathing

The lungs are well-adapted for exchange of gases:
- large surface area
- thin
- moist
- rich blood supply.

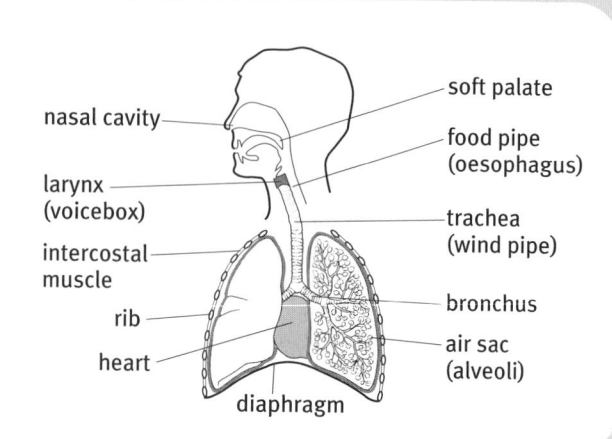

Labels on diagram: nasal cavity, larynx (voicebox), intercostal muscle, rib, heart, diaphragm, soft palate, food pipe (oesophagus), trachea (wind pipe), bronchus, air sac (alveoli)

Some of the oxygen in inhaled air passes into the blood stream and is carried by red blood cells to all cells of the body. These cells use oxygen in respiration to get energy out of food. The carbon dioxide has to be passed out of the blood into the lungs to be exhaled.

Inhalation	Exhalation
1 Ribs pulled up and out by muscles	1 Ribs moved down and in by muscles
2 Diaphragm pulled down by diaphragm muscles	2 Diaphragm goes up as diaphragm muscles relax
3 Chest volume increases because of 1 and 2	3 Chest volume decreases because of 1 and 2
4 Pressure inside chest decreases so air rushes into lungs	4 Pressure inside chest increases so air rushes out of lungs

	Air in %	Air out %
Oxygen	21	16
Carbon dioxide	0.04	4
Nitrogen	79	79
Water vapour	varies	large amounts

Carbon cycle

Carbon is a very important element in the molecules that make up living things, e.g. carbohydrates, fats and proteins. It is present in air and water, in large quantities, as carbon dioxide. It is constantly recycled through the environment which can be shown as the carbon cycle.

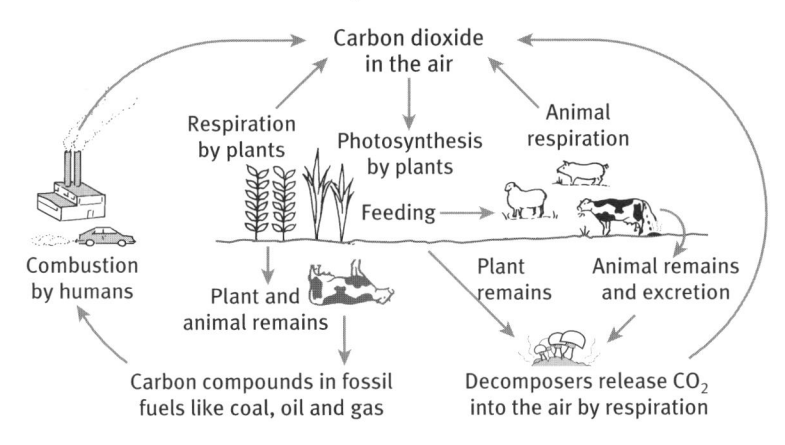

Cell division (mitosis)

In mitosis the chromosomes (containing DNA) in the nucleus are copied and pulled apart so that two new genetically identical cells are made. It is essential for growth and repair of tissues and is the basic process of asexual reproduction/cloning.

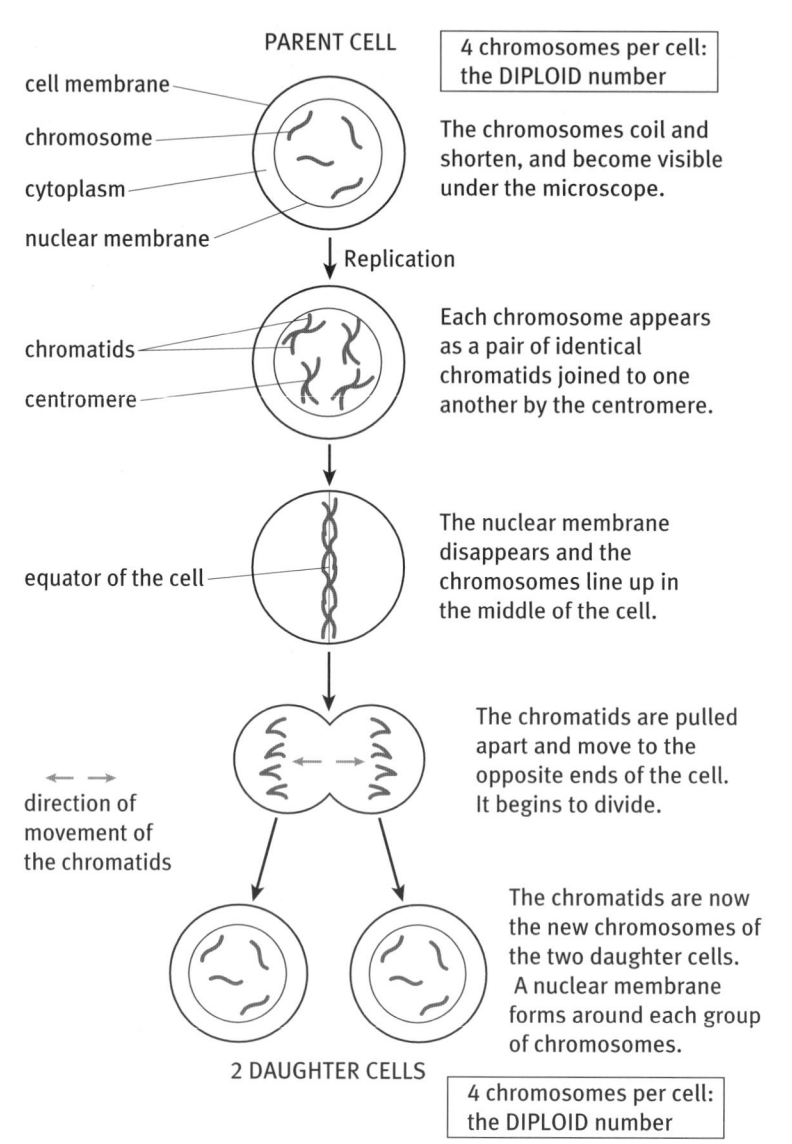

PARENT CELL

- cell membrane
- chromosome
- cytoplasm
- nuclear membrane

4 chromosomes per cell: the DIPLOID number

The chromosomes coil and shorten, and become visible under the microscope.

↓ Replication

- chromatids
- centromere

Each chromosome appears as a pair of identical chromatids joined to one another by the centromere.

- equator of the cell

The nuclear membrane disappears and the chromosomes line up in the middle of the cell.

← →
direction of movement of the chromatids

The chromatids are pulled apart and move to the opposite ends of the cell. It begins to divide.

2 DAUGHTER CELLS

The chromatids are now the new chromosomes of the two daughter cells. A nuclear membrane forms around each group of chromosomes.

4 chromosomes per cell: the DIPLOID number

Cell structure

The cell is the basic structure of all living things, except viruses.
Plant and animal cells have some parts in common and some differences.

Four things they both have in common.

Animal cell

1 **Nucleus** controls everything that goes on in the cell
2 **Cytoplasm** chemical reactions happen here
3 **Cell membrane** controls what goes in and out of the cell
4 **Mitochondria** convert glucose and oxygen into usable energy

Three additional structures

Plant cell

1 **Rigid cellulose cell wall** supports the cell
2 **Vacuole** – large space which contains cell sap, a weak solution of sugar and salts
3 **Chloroplasts** containing green chlorophyll for photosynthesis

Exam tip
You must know the names of the parts of animal and plant cells.

Cells, tissues and organs

- A group of **identical cells** is called a **tissue**.
- A group of **tissues** form an **organ**.
- A group of **organs** working together form an **organ system**.
- A group of **organ systems** form an **organism**.

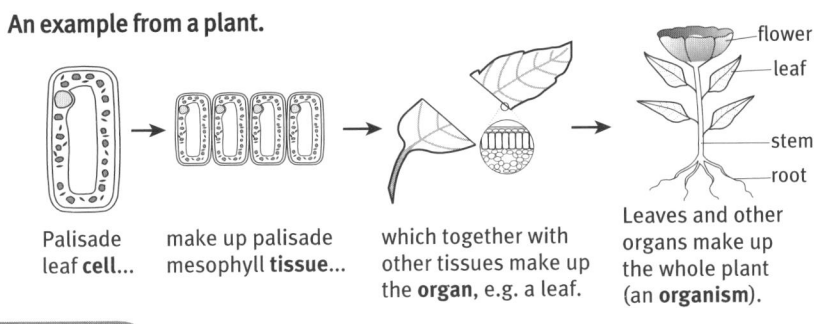

An example from a plant.

Palisade leaf **cell**... make up palisade mesophyll **tissue**... which together with other tissues make up the **organ**, e.g. a leaf. Leaves and other organs make up the whole plant (an **organism**).

flower
leaf
stem
root

Exam tip
Learn the names of some cells, organs and systems.

Chromosomes

- Chromosomes are threads of DNA (genetic material) coiled around a core of protein, found in the nucleus of cells. A gene is a short length of a chromosome.

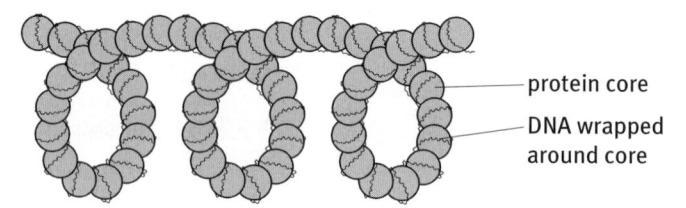

  - protein core
  - DNA wrapped around core

- They are only visible when a cell is dividing.
- Each species has a unique number of chromosomes.

Species	Number of chromosomes
Humans	46
Fruit flies	8
Mouse	40
Yeast	34

Circulation

Blood transports materials around the body. It flows from the heart in vessels called arteries, which branch and branch into smaller vessels. These capillaries within the tissues allow exchange of materials from blood to cells. The blood then flows back to the heart in larger vessels called veins. This is called the circulation, with the heart as the pump. The circulatory system actually has two main loops as shown in the diagram.

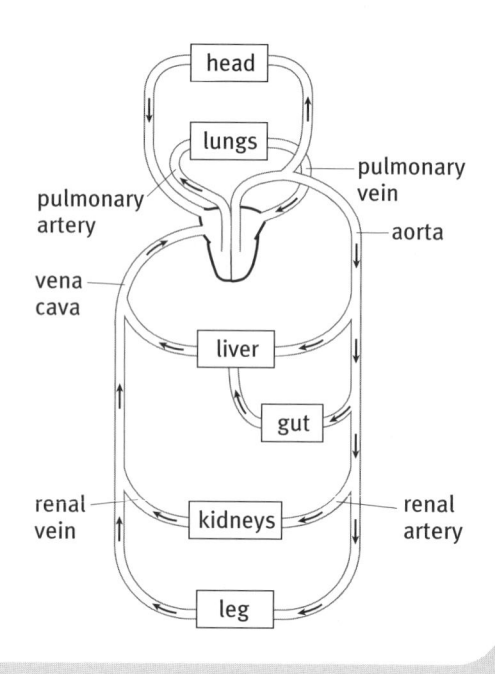

Exam tip

Remember: <u>A</u>rtery – <u>a</u>way, ve<u>in</u> – <u>in</u>.

Classification

Living things can be **classified** into a number of **taxonomic groups**. They are grouped according to the features they have in common. There are **five** main groups called Kingdoms.

```
                        Living things
    ┌───────────┬───────────┬───────────┬───────────┐
  Plants     Animals      Fungi      Monera      Protoctista
                                    (bacteria)  (protozoa + green algae)
```

These can be divided into smaller and smaller groups which have more and more features in common.

Exam tip

You have to know in detail the features of arthropods, plants and the vertebrates.

Cloning

Clones are genetically identical organisms. Many plants reproduce asexually on their own. **Clones** from plants can be made **artificially** by **micropropagation** and **tissue culture**. Traditionally this is done by cuttings, but new techniques use a small part of a plant like a bud or just a few cells and grow them in a special growth medium containing plant hormones, which stimulate cell division. The new cells differentiate into roots, shoots and leaves.

Cloning in **animals,** for example cows, involves splitting the cells of an early embryo (8-cell stage) and implanting them into several cows, where they grow.

See also
Asexual reproduction

Community

A community consists of all the populations of organisms living in a particular habitat at a particular point in time.

The community of a particular habitat will be made up of organisms which are specially adapted for that particular environment. In a woodland, for example, there may be populations of oak trees, hazel trees, bluebells, earthworms, wood beetles, blue tits, sparrowhawks, deer and many more.

Competition

All organisms compete for food and water, space to live in (territories), and mates to produce offspring with. Competition can be between members of the same species or between different species. The most successful organisms survive to pass on their genes to the next generation.

Consumer

An organism which **cannot make its own food** and feeds on other organisms is called a **consumer**. **All animals are consumers**. All plants are not, because they are producers and make their own food. Consumers may be:

- herbivores (plant eaters) e.g. rabbits, sheep, greenfly
- carnivores (only eat animals) e.g. eagles, lions
- omnivores (eat both plants and animals) e.g. humans, bears
- detritivores (eat the dead remains of plants and animals) e.g. earthworms, woodlice.

See also Food chains and webs

Decomposer

Decomposers are mostly the bacteria and fungi, which pour digestive enzymes onto the dead bodies of other organisms and then absorb the broken-down food. This causes the dead bodies to **putrefy**, i.e. rot.

The chemicals/minerals that are released from the dead organisms go back into the soil. They can be absorbed by plants and used to make important substances like proteins.

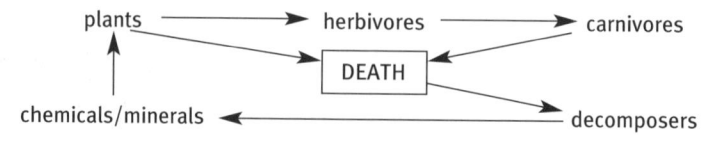

```
plants  ──────────▶  herbivores  ──────────▶  carnivores
                        │        DEATH        │
                        ▼          ▲          │
chemicals/minerals ◀────────────────── decomposers
        │                                      ▲
        └──────────────────────────────────────┘
```

Gardeners use decomposers in their compost heaps to decay garden waste. The decayed plant material is full of useful chemicals/minerals and can be used as natural organic fertilisers.

See also Bacteria, Fungi

Defence against disease

Microorganisms can enter our bodies in five ways.
1. Through the **skin and eyes**, particularly when damaged.
2. Through our **digestive system**, when contaminated food or drink is eaten.
3. Through the **respiratory system**, when contaminated air is breathed in.
4. Through the **reproductive system**, during sex if one or both partners have a sexually transmitted disease (STD).
5. Through **vectors**, e.g. mosquitoes carry the malaria parasite *Plasmodium* from person to person when they bite.

Our undamaged skin, chemicals in tears, mucus and cilia in our trachea, and our behaviour, e.g. cooking food well, boiling water, washing hands and preventing bites from insects all help prevent disease. Once microorganisms have entered our bodies they will reproduce rapidly unless they are destroyed by our immune system.

See also Immune system

Diet

A balanced diet must contain seven different types of **nutrients**.

	Contained in	Used for
Carbohydrates	bread/potatoes/cereals	energy
Proteins	meat/eggs/fish	making and repairing cells
Fats	cooking oil/margarine/cream	energy
Vitamins	fresh fruit/vegetables/cereal	making cells work properly
Minerals	e.g. iron in red meat/calcium in milk	iron for haemoglobin and calcium for bones and teeth
Fibre	fresh fruit and vegetables	stops constipation
Water	drinks and food	essential for staying alive

Digestion

Digestion is the breaking down of large insoluble molecules into small soluble ones, so that they can pass through the gut wall (in humans) into the blood stream. Enzymes break down big molecules to small ones.

See also Enzymes

Digestive system

This is the group of organs carrying out digestion and absorption of food.

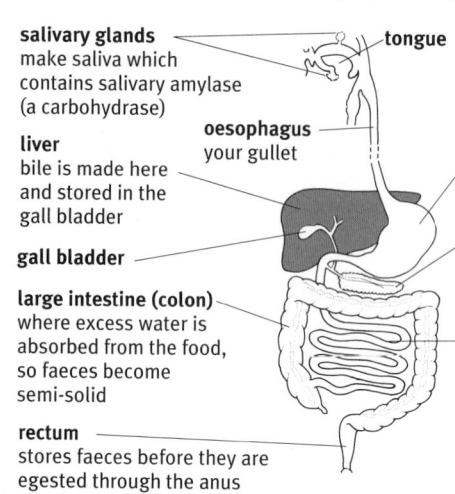

salivary glands
make saliva which contains salivary amylase (a carbohydrase)

tongue

oesophagus
your gullet

liver
bile is made here and stored in the gall bladder

gall bladder

large intestine (colon)
where excess water is absorbed from the food, so faeces become semi-solid

rectum
stores faeces before they are egested through the anus

stomach
1 the muscular stomach churns the food
2 it produces the protease enzyme (pepsin)
3 it produces hydrochloric acid
  a) to give the right pH for the pepsin enzyme to work and
  b) to kill bacteria

pancreas
produces all three enzymes: protease (trypsin), carbohydrase (pancreatic amylase) and lipase

small intestine
1 the lining produces all three enzymes: protease, carbohydrase and lipase
2 the inner surface is folded and covered with villi to increase the surface area
3 the digested 'food' is absorbed into the blood

Diseases

- **Infectious** or **contagious** diseases are caused by microorganisms, such as bacteria, viruses, fungi and protozoa. Disease-causing organisms are called **pathogens**.
- **Deficiency** diseases in plants and animals are caused by the **lack** of **essential nutrients** in their **diets**.

Nutrient lacking	Symptoms and effects
Magnesium in plants	Leaves can't make chlorophyll so go yellow, can't photosynthesise and plant will die.
Calcium in humans	Bones and teeth grow poorly and become brittle.
Iron in humans	Red blood cells don't have enough haemoglobin, so person suffers from anaemia.
Vitamin C in humans	Skin problems with the cracking and non-healing of wounds as in scurvy

- Some diseases can be **inherited**, e.g. haemophilia and cystic fibrosis. These genetic diseases are caused by a faulty gene, which is passed from parents to child in eggs and sperm (*see* **Genetic diseases** page 23).

See also Bacteria, Viruses, Fungi, Parasites and pathogens

DNA

- Our genes are made of **deoxyribonucleic acid** (DNA).
- It determines what we look like and how our cells work.
- It is a molecule which looks like a twisted ladder.
- It is called a **double helix**.
- The two strands are held together by bases called A (**adenine**), T (**thymine**), C (**cytosine**), and G (**guanine**).
- The sequence of bases on a DNA strand forms the **genetic code** of the organism.
- Three bases, a **codon**, give instructions for a particular amino acid, e.g. GGC codes for glycine, and AAG codes for lycine.
- Many amino acids are built up into proteins. These make up much of the content of cells and control what goes on.

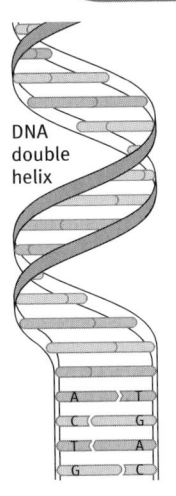

DNA double helix

Drugs use and misuse

Drugs are chemical substances which alter the way the body works. Some drugs used as medicines are useful, e.g. aspirin relieving pain and antibiotics such as penicillin. However, there are many drugs which are dangerous if misused, and many of them are **addictive** or habit-forming. They can cause long-term damage of the brain, liver and kidneys.

The loss of control and judgement caused by many drugs can easily lead to death from various causes, e.g. choking on vomit, car accidents, falling down stairs.

Group of drugs	Name of drugs	Effects on the body
stimulants	nicotine, cocaine, amphetamines, caffeine (in tea and coffee)	Produces feeling of boundless energy, but can cause dependence and changes in personality
depressants	alcohol, barbiturates, cannabis, solvents	Slows responses of nervous system and reduces awareness. Solvents, e.g. butane, can cause death on first try
analgesics (pain killers)	aspirin, heroin, morphine, codeine	Pain killer, produces feeling of well-being. Heroin/morphine are addictive and particularly destructive of personality

See also   Alcohol, Smoking

Ecosystem

This term describes a habitat, the community of plants, animals and micro-organisms that lives there and the physical (abiotic) factors that affect it. The diagram shows some of the interactions by arrows.

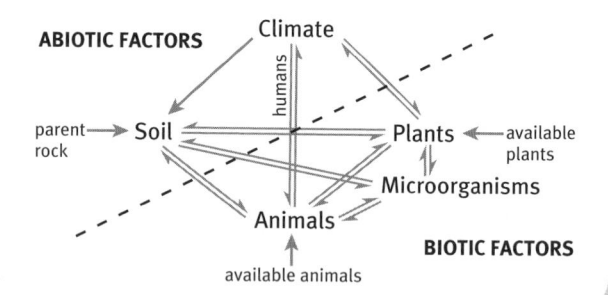

Environment

The environment of an organism is its **surroundings** in its **habitat**. It consists of:
- **physical** (**abiotic**) factors like temperature, light and soil
- **biotic** factors which are the living things, for example, predators.

Some environments are extreme like hot and cold deserts and organisms are specially adapted to survive there. Every organism has its own special niche within a habitat.

See also Competition, Consumer

Enzymes

- Enzymes are protein molecules.
- They control all the chemical reactions in living cells, e.g. photosynthesis, respiration and digestion.
- They speed up chemical reactions without being changed themselves. Digestive enzymes break down big molecules into small ones, which can then pass through the gut wall into the blood (see page 13).

1 Carbohydrases, e.g. amylase, convert starch to simple sugars.

$$\text{Starch} \xrightarrow{\text{carbohydrase}} \text{Glucose}$$

2 Proteases, e.g. pepsin, convert proteins to amino acids.

$$\text{Protein} \xrightarrow{\text{protease}} \text{Amino acids}$$

3 Lipases convert fats to fatty acids and glycerol.

$$\text{Fat} \xrightarrow{\text{lipases}} \textbf{Fatty acids} \text{ and } \textbf{Glycerol}$$

Evolution

The theory of evolution suggests that all the plants and animals on Earth gradually changed – **evolved** – over millions of years. Life on Earth began as simple organisms living in water, we think, about 3 000 000 000 years ago. All other living things have evolved from them. Some species die out, but new ones appear. We can trace the evolution of some species in the fossil record. **Natural selection** is the driving force of evolution.

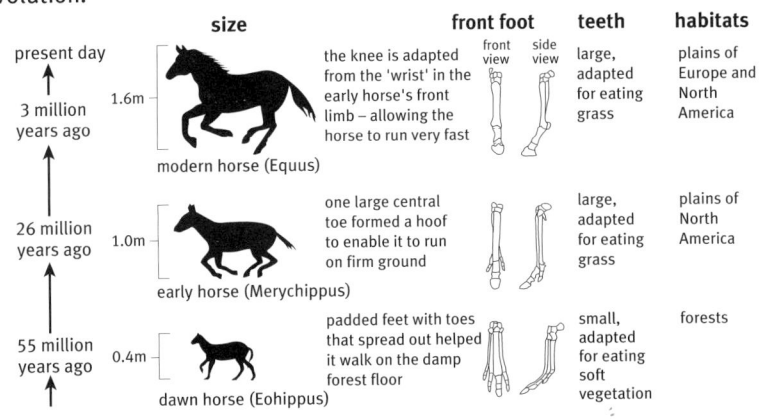

time	size		front foot	teeth	habitats
present day ↑ 3 million years ago	1.6m	modern horse (Equus)	the knee is adapted from the 'wrist' in the early horse's front limb – allowing the horse to run very fast (front view, side view)	large, adapted for eating grass	plains of Europe and North America
↑ 26 million years ago	1.0m	early horse (Merychippus)	one large central toe formed a hoof to enable it to run on firm ground	large, adapted for eating grass	plains of North America
↑ 55 million years ago	0.4m	dawn horse (Eohippus)	padded feet with toes that spread out helped it walk on the damp forest floor	small, adapted for eating soft vegetation	forests

See also   Fossils, Natural selection

Eye

- The **retina** is where light rays are focused. It is the **light sensitive** part containing **rods and cones**.
- **Rods** detect **dim light** but only respond in **black and white**.
- **Cones** are sensitive to **colours** and are concentrated in the **fovea**.
- The **pupil** is a **hole** in the middle of the **iris** which lets the **light go through**. It is **small in bright light** and **large in dim light**.
- The **aqueous humour** is a **runny clear liquid** and the **vitreous humour** is a **clear jelly**. They help the eye keep its shape.

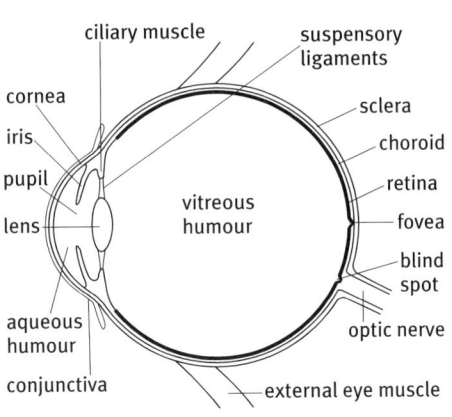

Labels: ciliary muscle, suspensory ligaments, cornea, sclera, iris, choroid, pupil, retina, lens, vitreous humour, fovea, blind spot, aqueous humour, optic nerve, conjunctiva, external eye muscle

Fertilisation

Fertilisation happens when **male** and **female sex cells** (gametes) meet up and fuse to make a **zygote**. This can divide and grow into a new individual. In human eggs and sperm there are **23 chromosomes**, half the number that normal body cells have. The fertilised egg (zygote) has **46**.

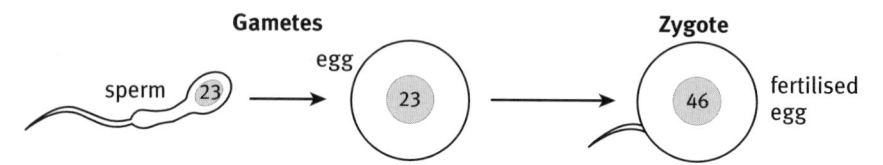

Gametes

sperm 23 → egg 23 → **Zygote** 46 fertilised egg

In flowering plants fertilisation happens after pollination when male gametes in pollen fuse with female gametes in ovules.

Fertilisers

Fertilisers contain essential **mineral nutrients** for plants. They are put on soil so plants can absorb them through their roots and grow better. The three main minerals are:

- nitrates (N)
- phosphates (P)
- potassium (K)

Fertilisers can be made in a chemical works (inorganic fertiliser) or be found in natural sources such as compost or manure (organic fertiliser). There can be a problem if too much fertiliser runs off fields into rivers and lakes. It is called **eutrophication** and can cause the death of most of the animals and plants in the water.

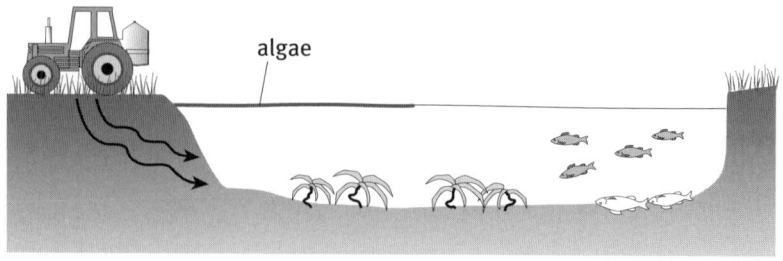

algae

Excess nitrate leaches into river or lake causing rapid growth of plants and algae.

Some plants start dying because they don't get enough light.

The microbes that rot the dead plants increase and use up all the oxygen in the water. This causes death of fish etc.

Flowers, fruits and seeds

Flowers contain the **reproductive organs** of plants. After **pollination** (transfer of gametes) and **fertilisation** (fusion of gametes) the flower develops into the **fruit** containing the **seeds**.

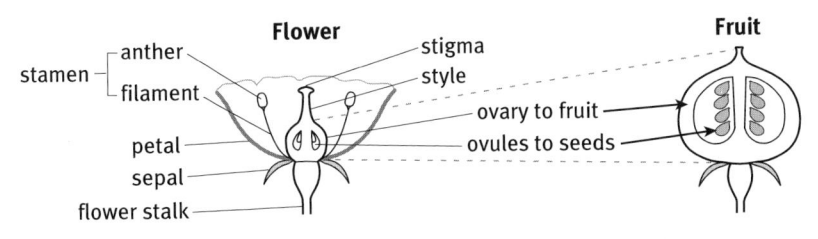

Flower: stamen (anther, filament), petal, sepal, flower stalk, stigma, style, ovary to fruit, ovules to seeds — **Fruit**

Food chains and webs

A food chain of organisms shows the feeding relationships between them. They start with a **producer** which uses the Sun's energy to make its own food. Arrows link the organisms and show where the energy goes from the producer to the consumers.

oak leaves	→	greenflies (aphids)	→	bluetit	→	sparrowhawk
producer		**primary consumer**		**secondary consumer**		**tertiary consumer**

A **food web** is a diagram to show the feeding relationships between different species in a community.

A woodland food web

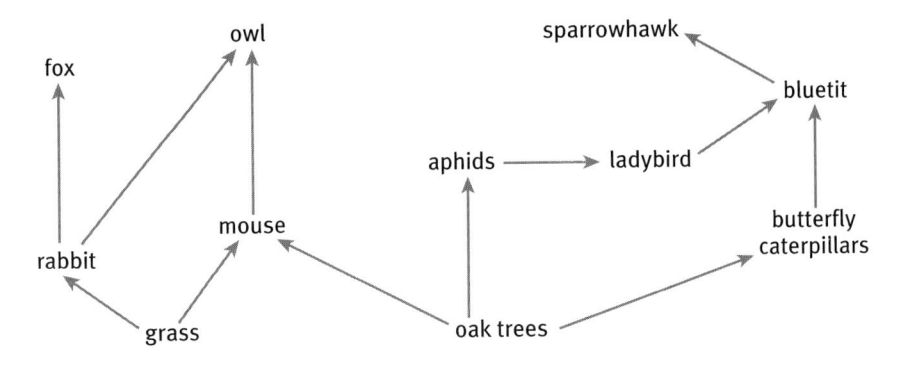

fox, owl, sparrowhawk, bluetit, aphids, ladybird, mouse, butterfly caterpillars, rabbit, grass, oak trees

See also   Consumer, Producer, Pyramids of numbers and biomass

Food production (farming)

Farming is important to humans because it allows us to make a lot of food from less land. Modern methods produce plenty of food but can damage the environment. Here are some of the problems.

- Careless use of **fertilisers** can cause **eutrophication**.
- **Pesticides** disturb food chains and reduce insect, bird and mammal populations as they get concentrated along the food chains.
- Removal of hedges and trees (**deforestation**) destroys the habitat of wild life and can lead to serious soil erosion.
- **Intensively rearing animals**, e.g. battery chickens, is thought to be cruel by some people.

Some farming methods have positive benefits. Here are some examples.

- **Organic farming** uses traditional methods to produce food without the use of artificial chemicals.
- Managed **salmon** and **trout farms** rear fish in a **controlled** way.
- **Glass houses** have advantages for commercial food growing, by being able to control the environment so easily, e.g. temperature and light.

Food tests

- The **iodine test** for **starch**. A few drops of iodine on starch turns from:

    brown → **blue/black** (no heating).

- The **Biuret test** for **protein**. The Biuret solution made of dilute sodium hydroxide solution and dilute copper sulphate solution, with protein goes from:

    pale blue → **purple** (no heating).

- The **Benedict's test** for **simple sugars**. The bright clear blue Benedict's solution when boiled with a simple sugar goes from:

    bright blue → **orange-red precipitate**.

- The **alcohol-emulsion test** for **fats**. Alcohol is shaken with fat/oil and then poured into a tube of water. Fat is shown by a change from:

    clear colourless → **white emulsion** (no heating).

Fossils

Fossils are the preserved and ancient remains of living things.
- They give clues about the history of life.
- Fossils are rare as dead organisms usually rot.

Fossils can be formed by the dead plant or animal being:
- trapped in sediment which turned to rock
- trapped in amber, e.g. insects
- frozen in ice
- preserved in acid bogs.

See also **Evolution**

Fossil fuels

Fossil fuels are **coal, oil** and **natural gas**. We burn them to release the **energy** they contain. In power stations the heat they make turns water to steam, which turns turbines to produce electricity. Petrol from oil also powers cars. They release gases when burned. **Carbon dioxide** is a major air **pollutant**, causing an increased **greenhouse effect**. **Sulphur dioxide** and **nitrogen oxides** are a major cause of **acid rain**.

Alternative energy sources use for example wind and wave energy, which are less polluting.

Fungi

The fungi form a Kingdom on their own. Along with bacteria they are responsible for the **decay** and **decomposition** of **dead organic matter**.
- They are made up of **slender tubes** called **hyphae**.
- The mass of hyphae which form an individual is called the **mycelium**.
- Fruiting bodies, e.g. mushrooms, produce **spores**.
- Each spore has some cytoplasm and a few nuclei and can grow into a new mycelium.
- A special fungus called **yeast** is made of oval cells. It is used by humans in bread, wine and beer making and by genetic engineers (see page 24).

Genetic diagrams and inheritance

Genetic diagrams show how genes are passed from one generation to the next. Most animals and plants have **two genes** which can affect a particular characteristic. They are on different chromosomes which get separated during **meiosis**. **Sex cells** therefore only have **one** of the **genes**. After sex cells fuse the **fertilised egg** has **two genes** again.

It is best to show this using a diagram like one of these:

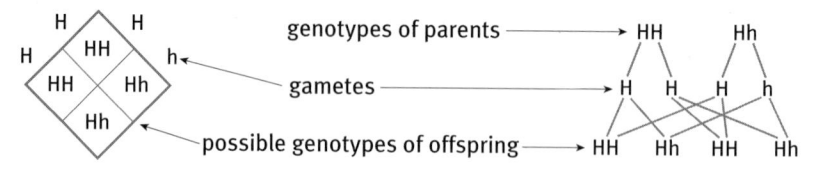

genotypes of parents → HH   Hh

gametes → H H   H h

possible genotypes of offspring → HH Hh HH Hh

To follow genetic diagrams there are many words to learn and understand.

- **Allele** is just another name for a **gene**. If you have two versions of a gene, like H and h, then they are called alleles instead of genes.
- **Genotype** is just what type of genes you've got, e.g. HH, Hh, or hh.
- **Phenotype** is what **physical characteristics** result from the genotype.
- A **dominant allele** shown by a capital letter, e.g. H dominates the **recessive allele** shown by a small letter, e.g. h.
- **Homozygous** genotypes have the same alleles, i.e. hh or HH.
- **Heterozygous** genotypes have different alleles, i.e. Hh.

Here is an example of a cross between a hairy mouse (HH) and a bald hairless mouse (hh). It is called a **monohybrid cross** as it involves one pair of alleles in each parent.

Parents'	Phenotype	Hairy	x	Bald
	Genotype	HH		hh
	Gametes (sex cells)	H or H		h or h
Offsprings'	Genotype	Hh Hh		Hh Hh
	Phenotype		all Hairy	

If two of these mice now breed they will produce a second generation with the following possibilities.

Parents'	Phenotype	Hairy	x	Hairy
	Genotype	Hh		Hh
	Gametes	H or h		H or h
Offsprings'	Genotype	HH Hh		hH hh
	Phenotype	Hairy Hairy		Hairy Bald

This gives a 3:1 **ratio** of hairy to bald offspring in the second generation.

Genetic diseases

Some diseases can be **inherited**. They include **cystic fibrosis, sickle cell anaemia, muscular dystrophy** and **haemophilia**. The last two are described as being sex-linked.

- **Cystic fibrosis** affects 1 in 1600 people in the UK. It causes sticky mucus in the lungs, which get damaged after repeated infections. There are digestive problems too. Cystic fibrosis is caused by a recessive gene (c) and is carried by about **1 person in 15**. The genetic diagram shows how the gene is passed on.

This diagram shows that there is a **1 in 4 chance** of a child having the disease, if **both parents are carriers**.

Parents' **phenotype**	normal, but carrier	normal, but carrier
Parents' **genotype**	Cc	Cc
Gametes'	C c	C c
Offsprings' **genotype**	CC Cc cC cc	
Offsprings' **phenotype**	normal carrier carrier Cystic fibrosis sufferer	

- **Sickle cell anaemia** is also caused by a recessive gene.
- **Haemophilia** causes a problem with blood clotting. It is caused by a faulty gene on the X-**chromosome**. As females have two X-chromosomes they have two chances of having the normal blood clotting gene. Males with one X- and one Y-chromosome have only one allele for blood clotting so it is a disease linked with being male. The same is true of **muscular dystrophy**.

The genetics of haemophilia and other sex-linked diseases

Example: the bloodclotting allele (H or h), there are five possible combinations.

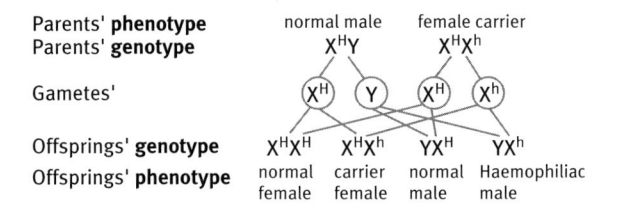

Parents' **phenotype**	normal male	female carrier
Parents' **genotype**	X^HY	X^HX^h
Gametes'	X^H Y	X^H X^h
Offsprings' **genotype**	X^HX^H X^HX^h YX^H YX^h	
Offsprings' **phenotype**	normal carrier normal Haemophiliac female female male male	

1. Normal male X^HY
2. Haemophiliac male X^hY
3. Normal female X^HX^H
4. Carrier female X^HX^h
5. Haemophiliac female (rarely develops) X^hX^h

The genotypes for any sex-linked genes must indicate the X and Y (chromosomes) as well as the H and h (genes).

Genetic engineering

This is quite a new science. The basic idea is to cut out a gene from one organism and put it in another, usually a microorganism, which can then make a useful protein, e.g. human insulin is made by genetically modified (GM) bacteria. As well as medicines, enzymes like chymosin for making vegetarian cheese can be made by genetic engineering.

There is much debate about genetically modifying food plants.

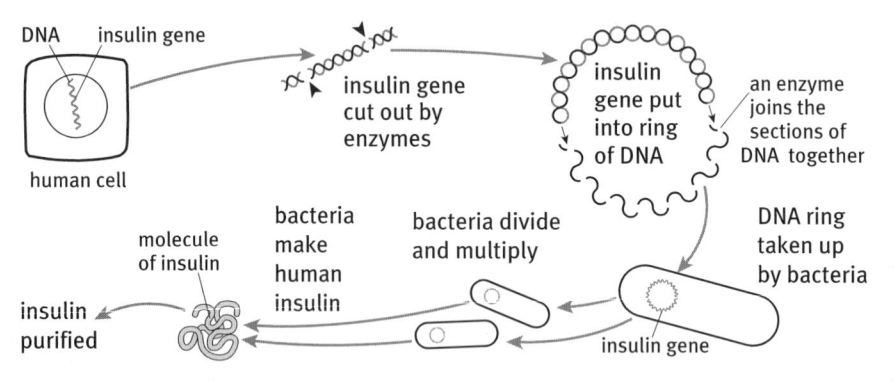

Germination

Germination is when seeds start to grow. The seeds will stay **dormant** until the **conditions** around them are suitable for germination. There are three things that seeds need:

1 A suitable temperature.
2 Oxygen.
3 Enough water.

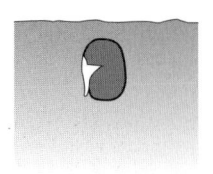

Bean takes in water and starts to grow using food stores.

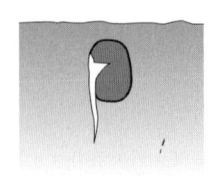

Root develops first and takes in water.

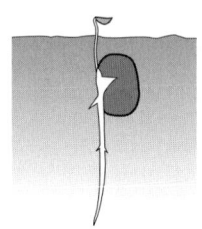

Shoot begins to grow and leaves develop so plant starts to make own food.

Greenhouse effect and global warming

The **greenhouse effect** is a **natural process** which keeps enough **heat** trapped in our atmosphere to **support life**. There are several different gases that keep heat in, e.g. **carbon dioxide** (CO_2) and **methane**.

The problem of global warming is caused because we are **burning** so many **fossil fuels** to provide energy for a growing human population. The extra CO_2 plus methane from **growing rice** and **rearing cows** along with **deforestation** means that the average global temperature is going up. This may lead to changing weather patterns and **melting ice-caps**, so that **rising sea levels** could cause **flooding**.

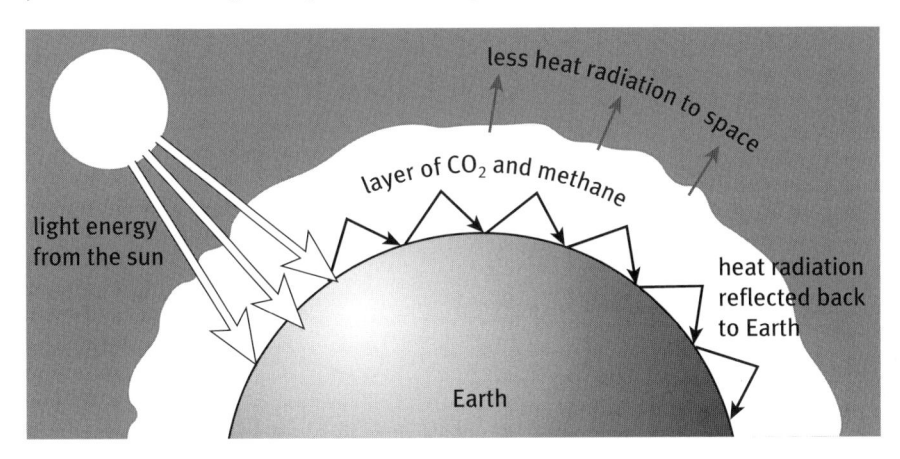

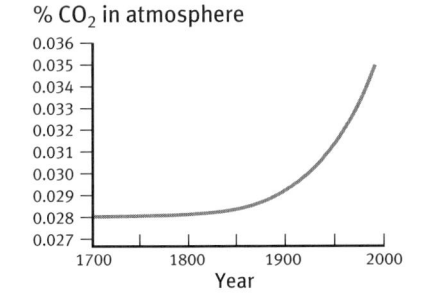

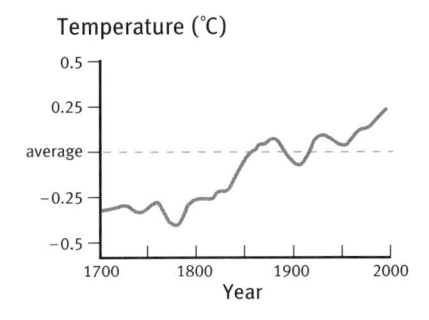

less heat radiation to space

layer of CO_2 and methane

light energy from the sun

heat radiation reflected back to Earth

Earth

% CO_2 in atmosphere (1700–2000)

Temperature (°C) (1700–2000)

Habitat

The place where an organism lives is called its habitat, e.g. a woodland or a pond.

See also Environment

Heart

The heart is made of special muscle. It is a double pump.

- The **right atrium** of the heart receives **deoxygenated blood** from the body via the **venae cavae**.
- The **right ventricle** pumps this blood to the **lungs** via the **pulmonary artery**.
- The **left atrium** receives **oxygenated blood** from the lungs via the **pulmonary vein**.
- The **left ventricle** pumps this blood round the **whole body** via the **aorta**.
- The right side of the heart has **thinner** walls than the left as it pumps the blood only a short distance to the lungs. The left side pumps blood around the whole body and therefore has more muscular, **thicker** walls.
- The ventricles pump the blood around the body and are bigger than the atria which pump blood only to the ventricles.
- Valves are present to make sure blood flows in one direction only.

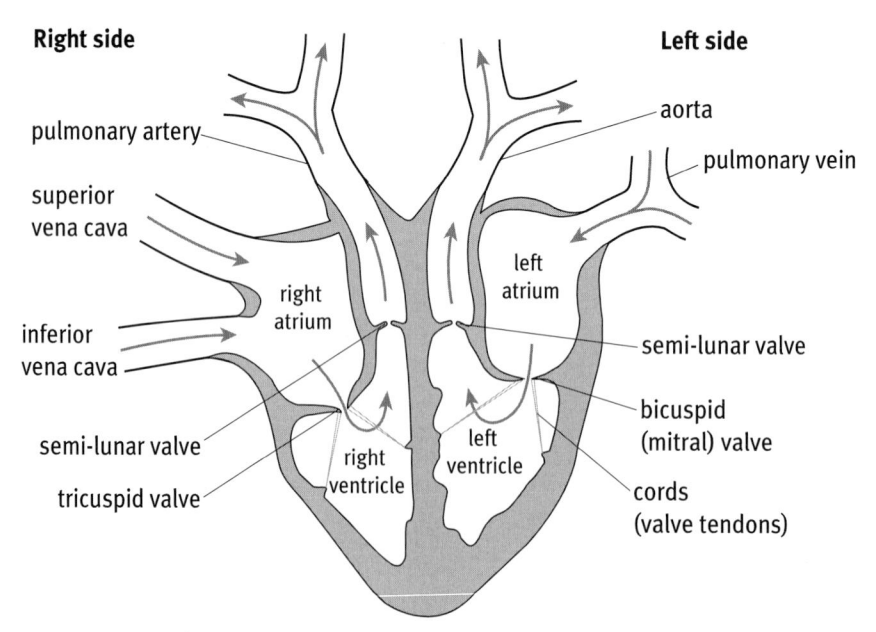

Right side

- pulmonary artery
- superior vena cava
- inferior vena cava
- right atrium
- semi-lunar valve
- tricuspid valve
- right ventricle

Left side

- aorta
- pulmonary vein
- left atrium
- semi-lunar valve
- bicuspid (mitral) valve
- left ventricle
- cords (valve tendons)

The arrow shows the direction of the flow of blood.

See also Circulation

Homeostasis

Homeostasis means keeping a **constant internal environment**.
There are six different bodily levels that need to be controlled.

1. Removal of waste CO_2.
2. Removal of waste urea.
3. Ion content, e.g. chloride ions (Cl^-).
4. Water content.
5. Sugar content.
6. Temperature.

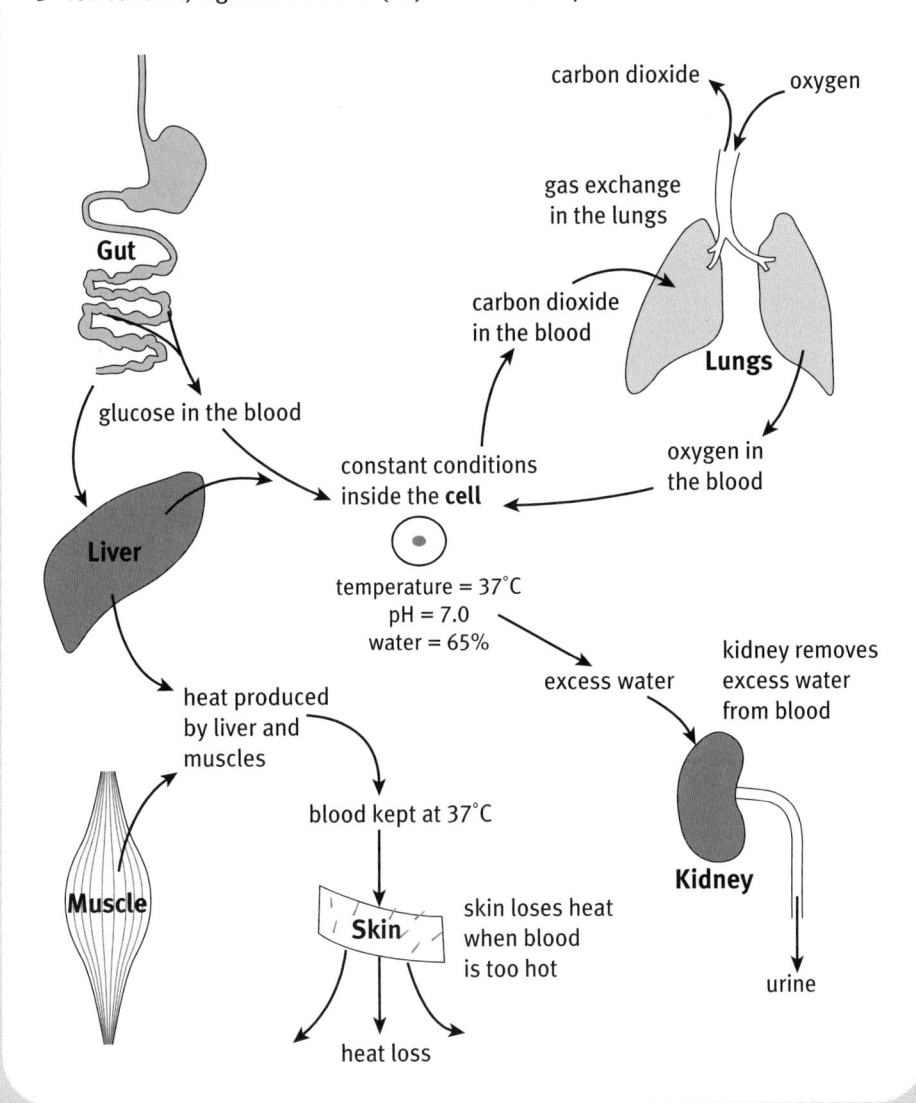

carbon dioxide
oxygen

gas exchange in the lungs

Gut

carbon dioxide in the blood

Lungs

glucose in the blood

oxygen in the blood

Liver

constant conditions inside the **cell**

temperature = 37°C
pH = 7.0
water = 65%

excess water

kidney removes excess water from blood

heat produced by liver and muscles

blood kept at 37°C

Muscle

Skin

skin loses heat when blood is too hot

Kidney

urine

heat loss

Hormones (endocrine system)

Hormones are chemicals made in ductless glands in the body. They are released directly into the blood and travel all over the body. Certain target cells can **pick up** the chemicals which then do something in response. Hormones are part of the endocrine system, which is very important in controlling things that need constant adjustment. Some have long-term effects, e.g. on puberty.

An important hormone is **insulin,** which along with the hormone **glucagon** controls the level of blood sugar (glucose).

high blood → pancreas → **insulin** → liver → glucose turns → normal blood
sugar   [endocrine gland]   [target organ]   to glycogen   sugar

low blood → pancreas → **glucagon** → liver → glycogen turns → normal blood
sugar   to glucose   sugar

Diabetes is a disease in which the pancreas doesn't make enough insulin. This can be fatal. The problem can be controlled by injecting insulin before meals and being careful with carbohydrate intake in the diet.

Immune system

Once microorganisms like **bacteria** and **viruses** have entered our bodies they reproduce and can make us feel ill. Our **immune system** is triggered to destroy them. There are **two** main **white blood** cells involved:

- **phagocytes** ingest microorganisms

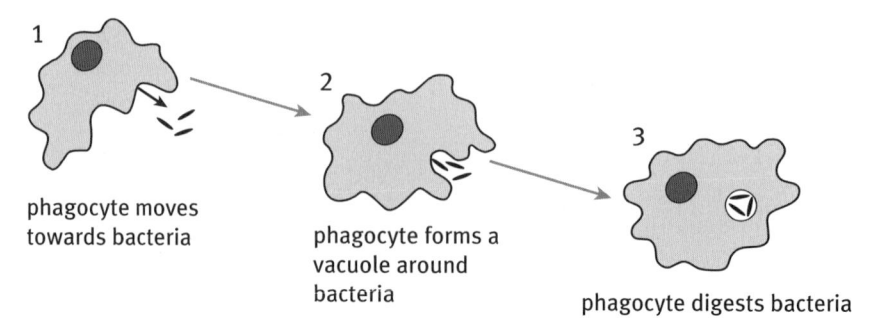

1. phagocyte moves towards bacteria
2. phagocyte forms a vacuole around bacteria
3. phagocyte digests bacteria

- **lymphocytes** make proteins called **antibodies**. These can destroy the invading organisms (**antigens**) or the poisons (**toxins**) they make. Each type of antigen and toxin has its own type of antibody.

tetanus bacteria invade the body

lymphocyte

lymphocytes make antibodies and release them into the blood

antibodies clump bacteria together

phagocyte

bacteria are ingested by phagocyte

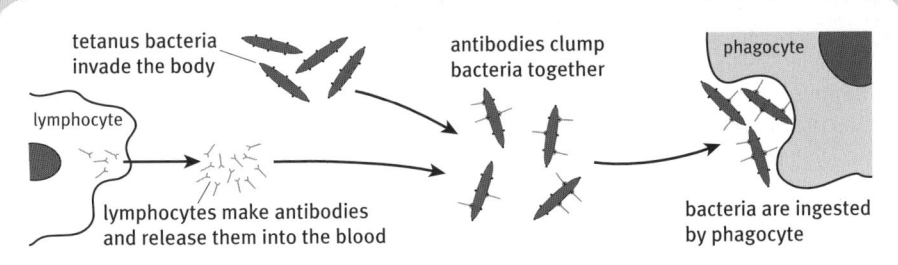

It takes time to make enough antibodies to kill all the disease organisms, but if the same bacteria or viruses invade again, the body can kill them straight away before you feel ill. You have **natural immunity**.

Immunisation (vaccination)

Immunisation involves injecting **dead microorganisms** into the body. This causes **lymphocytes** to make **antibodies** against them. The microorganisms can't cause harm because they are dead. If later live microorganisms of the same type enter the body they are killed immediately by the pre-made antibodies. The liquid containing the dead microorganism is called a **vaccine**. It is not possible to produce vaccines against all microbes, e.g. the virus that causes the common cold. This is because microbes reproduce so fast that new, slightly different varieties appear.

Keys

Keys are used to identify creatures. They involve a series of questions which all have two possible answers. The two answers divide a group into two parts. Further questions continue to divide the group up until just one is left.

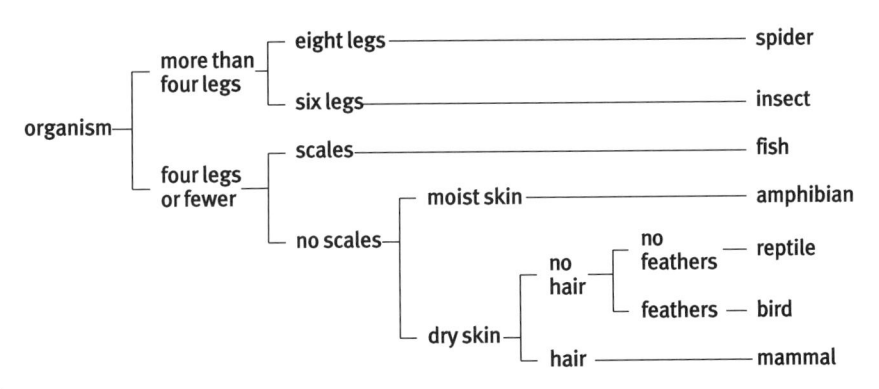

organism
- more than four legs
  - eight legs —————————— spider
  - six legs —————————— insect
- four legs or fewer
  - scales —————————— fish
  - no scales
    - moist skin —————————— amphibian
    - dry skin
      - no hair
        - no feathers — reptile
        - feathers — bird
      - hair —————————— mammal

Kidneys

Humans have two kidneys, which act as filters to **clean the blood**. They do three main jobs.

1. Remove urea from the blood.
2. Adjust the concentration of ions such as sodium and chloride in the blood.
3. Adjust the water content of the blood.

There are about a million nephrons in each kidney. Each nephron is a filtration unit. After blood is filtered under pressure into the nephron, useful substances are reabsorbed, urine is made and excreted via the bladder.

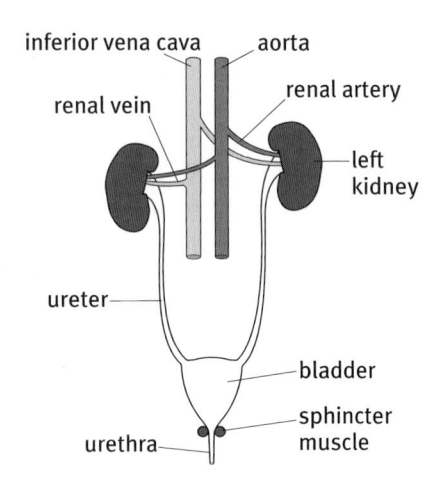

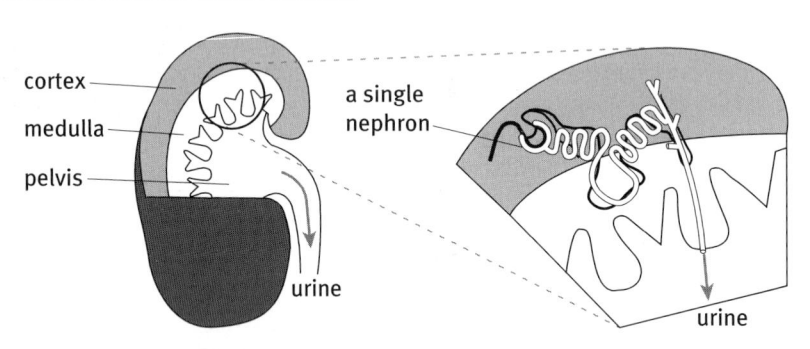

Life processes *(characteristics of living things)*

There are **seven** things that all living things must do to be **alive**. These are called **life processes**.

1. **M**ovement
2. **R**eproduction
3. **S**ensitivity
4. **G**rowth
5. **R**espiration
6. **E**xcretion
7. **N**utrition

They can be remembered by the mnemonic **MRS GREN**

Limiting factors

A process like **photosynthesis** has several things which affect how fast it works, e.g. amount of **light**, amount of **carbon dioxide** and **temperature**. At any one time one of these factors must be stopping the process going faster. On warm, bright days carbon dioxide will be limiting photosynthesis (see graph), whilst on cool, dull days temperature or light may be limiting.

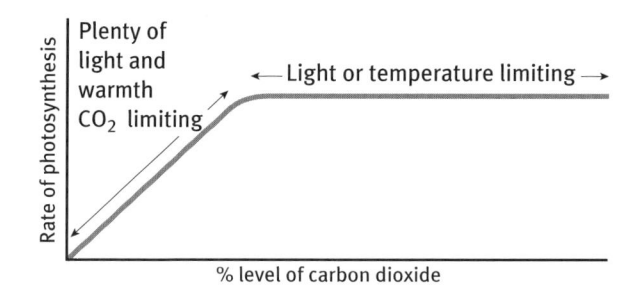

Rate of photosynthesis vs % level of carbon dioxide: Plenty of light and warmth, CO_2 limiting ← Light or temperature limiting →

Meiosis

Meiosis is a special type of cell division which is responsible for making sex cells (gametes). In humans it happens in the **ovaries** and **testes**. Each diploid cell with 23 pairs of chromosomes that undergoes meiosis makes four new haploid cells, each with a single set of chromosomes, i.e. 23.

1. This testis cell is about to divide by meiosis. The chromosomes are visible inside the nucleus.

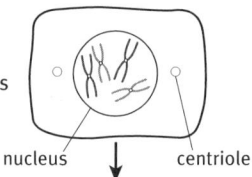

2. The homologous chromosomes pair up.

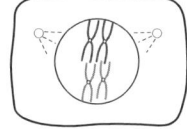

3. The pairs of chromosomes line up in the middle of the cell on the spindle fibres.

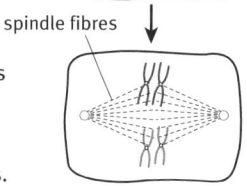

4. The homologous pairs of chromosomes are pulled apart. Half of the chromosomes go to each side of the cell.

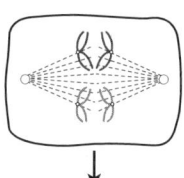

5. The cell first divides into two cells.

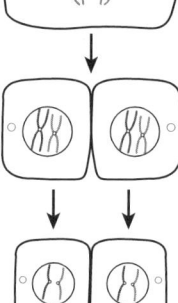

6. Then the two cells divide again as the chromatids are pulled apart. This forms four new cells which then develop into sperm.

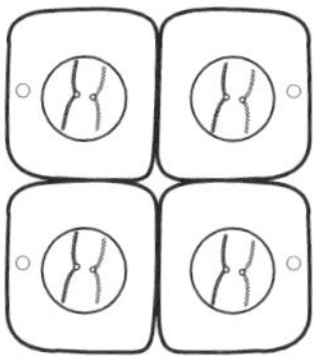

Menstrual cycle (oestrogen and progesterone)

The menstrual cycle has four stages.

1. Day 1 is when a **period** (bleeding) starts. The lining of the uterus breaks down for about 3 to 5 days.
2. The lining of the womb builds up again, from day 5 to day 14 ready to receive a fertilised egg.
3. At day 14 a ripe egg is released from the ovary (ovulation).
4. The lining continues to develop for another 14 days, until day 28. If no fertilised egg has embedded in the uterus lining by day 28 then the spongy lining starts to break down again and the whole cycle starts over.

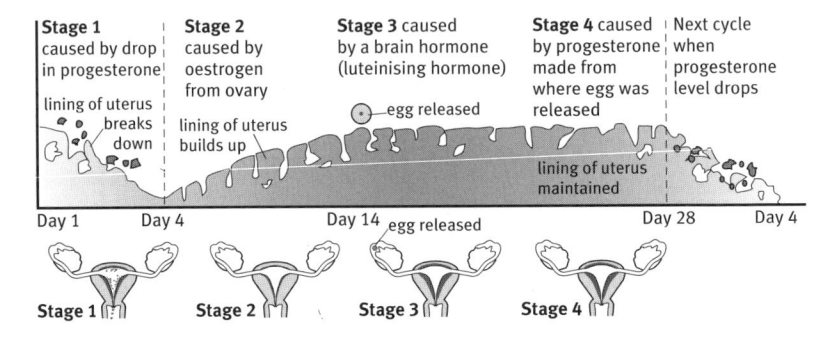

Stage 1 caused by drop in progesterone — lining of uterus breaks down

Stage 2 caused by oestrogen from ovary — lining of uterus builds up

Stage 3 caused by a brain hormone (luteinising hormone) — egg released

Stage 4 caused by progesterone made from where egg was released — lining of uterus maintained

Next cycle when progesterone level drops

Day 1   Day 4   Day 14 egg released   Day 28   Day 4

Stage 1   Stage 2   Stage 3   Stage 4

Oestrogen and **progesterone** are the two main hormones in the menstrual cycle. They are produced in the **ovaries** and control the main events of the cycle.

- Oestrogen makes the **lining of the uterus thicken** and **grow**. It stimulates the brain to make luteinising hormone which triggers the release of an egg at day 14.
- Progesterone maintains the lining of the uterus. When the level falls, the lining breaks down. (N.B. During pregnancy the progesterone level stays high.) The contraceptive pill causes the body to behave as though it's pregnant – extra progesterone means no egg is released.

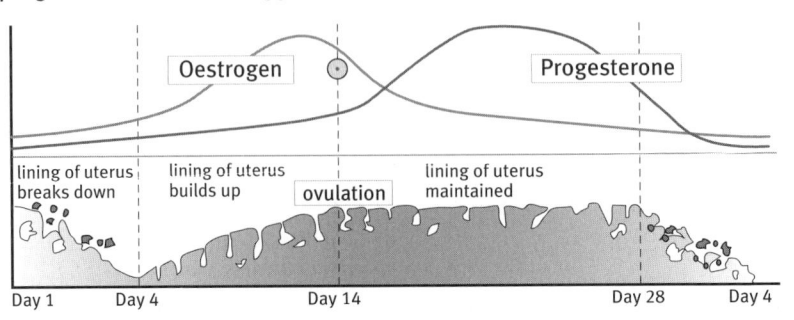

Oestrogen   Progesterone

lining of uterus breaks down | lining of uterus builds up | ovulation | lining of uterus maintained

Day 1   Day 4   Day 14   Day 28   Day 4

Movement (skeleton and muscles)

The functions of the skeleton are:
- protection • support • movement.

It is made of many **bones** which move against each other at **joints**. There are different kinds of joint. The two main ones are **hinge joints** (e.g. knee) and **ball and socket joints** (e.g. shoulder). These **freely movable joints** are lubricated by synovial fluid and the ends of bones protected by cartilage.

Antagonistic muscles work in pairs.

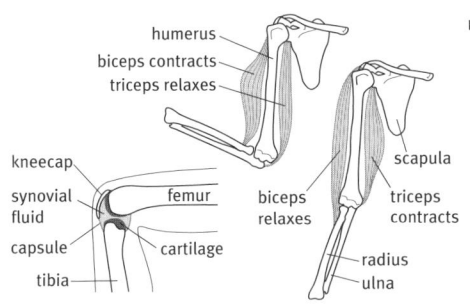

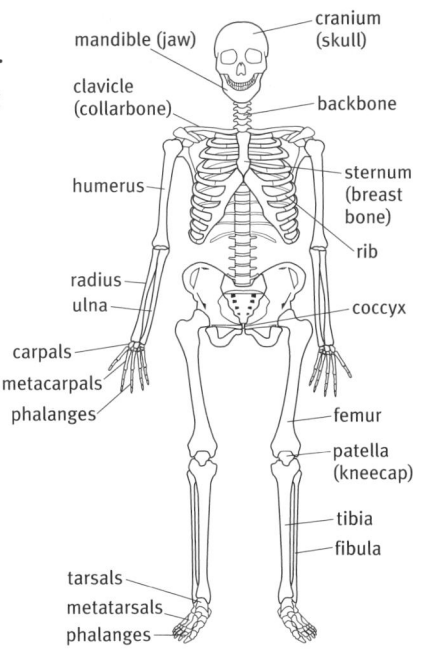

Movement in and out of cells

- **Diffusion** is the movement of particles from an area of high concentration to an area of low concentration. In living things it is important, for example, in the movement of **gases** in and out of **leaves** and of **oxygen** from **lungs** into blood and **carbon dioxide** from blood into lungs.

- **Osmosis** is a special kind of diffusion. It is the movement of **water molecules** across a **partially permeable membrane** from a region of **high** water concentration to a region of **low** water concentration. **Osmosis** is very important because all cells have cell membranes which are partially permeable, so water moves in and out by osmosis. It is, for example, how water moves into root hair cells from the soil.

- Active transport is the movement of particles **against** a **concentration gradient**, i.e. low to high. It requires **energy**. This is important in the **movement** of ions like **nitrates** from soil water into **roots**. It is also essential, for example, in moving ions across **nerve** cell membranes so that they can **transmit nerve impulses**.

Mutation

A mutation occurs when an organism develops a sudden change in one or more of its characteristics. It is caused by a fault in the DNA. Most mutations are harmful, but sometimes the change is advantageous, e.g. antibiotic resistance gives some bacteria an advantage in a body being treated with antibiotics, allowing them to survive and pass resistance onto the next generation. This is **natural selection** and **evolution** at work.

Mutations can be caused by natural events, e.g. ultra-violet radiation or artificial events such as X-rays and exposure to chemical mutagens like those in cigarette smoke.

Natural selection

Darwin's theory of natural selection explains how the variety of life on Earth could have **evolved**.

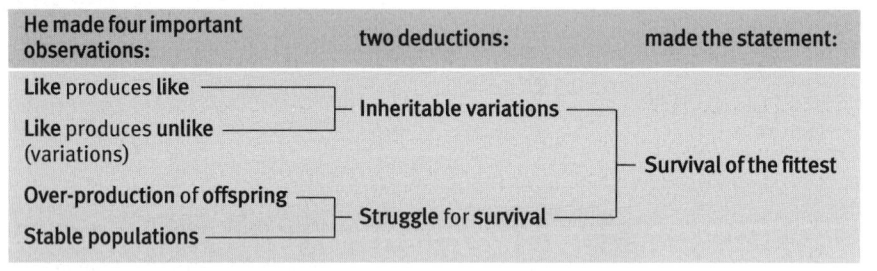

He made four important observations:	two deductions:	made the statement:
Like produces **like**	Inheritable variations	
Like produces **unlike** (variations)		Survival of the fittest
Over-production of offspring	Struggle for survival	
Stable populations		

The idea of **survival of the fittest** in which the strongest and most suited organisms to their environment pass on their genes to the next generation is the basis for **evolution**.

Nerve cells (neurones)

Neurones transmit **electrical impulses** very quickly around the body. The three types of neurone are:
- **sensory** neurone, which sends impulses into the central nervous system (CNS)
- **motor** neurone, which sends impulses from the CNS out to muscles and glands
- **relay** neurone, which links neurones in the CNS.

See also Reflexes

Nervous system

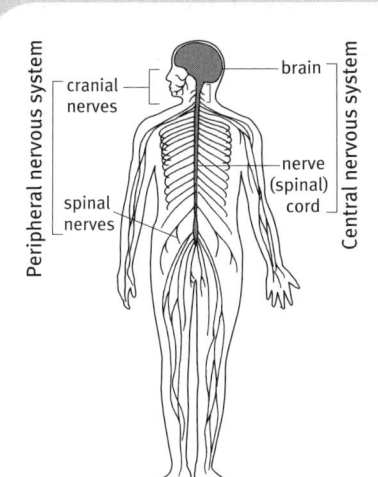

The nervous system is responsible for **coordination** within humans.

Sense organs and **receptors** react to stimuli and send **electrical impulses** to the **CNS** (**the brain** and **spinal cord**), where reflexes and actions are coordinated. Impulses are sent out from the CNS to **effectors** which respond appropriately.

Nitrogen cycle

This is very complex, but very important because plants need to absorb nitrogen in the form of nitrates from the soil so that they can make proteins for healthy growth.

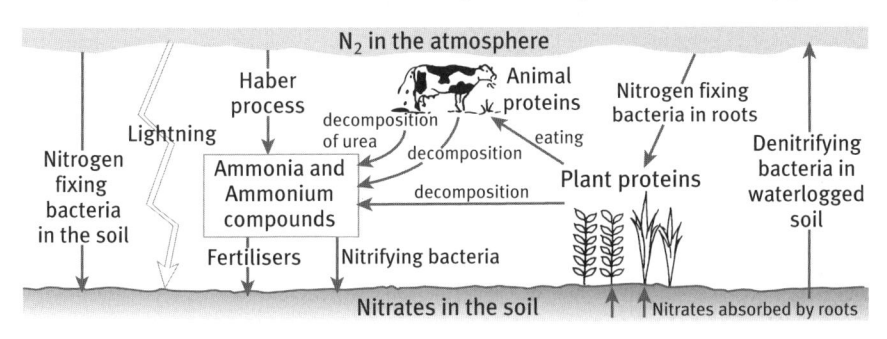

There are four different types of bacteria involved in the nitrogen cycle.
- **Putrefying bacteria** – these are decomposers which turn proteins and urea in dead organisms into ammonia or ammonium compounds.
- **Nitrifying bacteria** – these turn ammonium compounds in decaying matter into useful nitrates.
- **Nitrogen-fixing bacteria** – these turn useless nitrogen in the air into useful nitrates.
- **Denitrifying bacteria** – in boggy ground these are unhelpful because they turn nitrates back into nitrogen gas.

Ozone layer

- The ozone layer is high up in the atmosphere.
- It reacts with the harmful UV rays from the sun and stops a lot of them reaching the Earth's surface.
- The UV can damage the DNA in cells and cause mutations and cancer.
- Large holes in the ozone layer above the north and south poles are potentially very dangerous.
- It is believed that the holes have been caused by pollutant CFC gases, which are used as coolants in refrigeration and as propellants in spray cans.

Parasites and pathogens

- Organisms which live on or in another (the host) and cause the host harm are called parasites.
- They can be microorganisms or larger organisms such as tapeworms or fleas.
- Pathogens are disease-causing organisms.

Pest control

Common pests on crops are greenfly (aphids), whitefly, mealy bugs and red spider mites. They can be controlled with chemicals (**pesticides**). The advantages of using pesticides are:

- less loss of crops
- less damage to crops.

Disadvantages are many.

- Some pests are resistant to chemicals.
- The chemicals have been used repeatedly and in large amounts.
- They harm helpful insects such as ladybirds and bees as well as harmful ones.
- They can enter the human food chain.

Biological control methods employ **natural predators** of pests. For example, *Encarsia* is a tiny wasp which lays its eggs inside whitefly, who then get eaten from the inside. This is particularly useful in greenhouses.

Photosynthesis

Photosynthesis is the process that makes food (glucose) in plants. It takes place in the **green leaves** of plants. **Sunlight** energy is essential for the process and is absorbed by the green pigment **chlorophyll**. The raw materials are **carbon dioxide** and **water**. The products are **glucose** and **oxygen**.

The equation for photosynthesis is:

$$\text{carbon dioxide} + \text{water} \xrightarrow{\text{sunlight energy absorbed by chlorophyll}} \text{glucose} + \text{oxygen}$$

$$6CO_2 + 6H_2O \xrightarrow{\text{sunlight energy absorbed by chlorophyll}} C_6H_{12}O_6 + 6O_2$$

- Leaves are **broad** to provide a **large surface area** to trap lots of sunlight.
- **Palisade** cells are packed with chloroplasts which absorb light.
- **Guard cells** open and close stomata which allow gases into and out of the leaf.

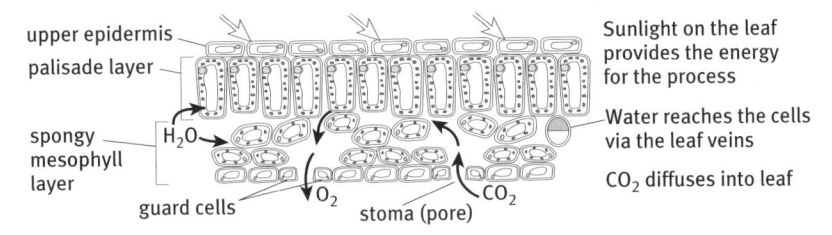

upper epidermis
palisade layer
spongy mesophyll layer
guard cells
H_2O
O_2
stoma (pore)
CO_2

Sunlight on the leaf provides the energy for the process
Water reaches the cells via the leaf veins
CO_2 diffuses into leaf

Plant hormones

Plants produce **chemicals** which affect **growth** and **development**. **Auxins** are made in the growing tips of plants and diffuse back to stimulate cells to get longer. They are also responsible for plants being able to respond to light, gravity and moisture. These growth movements are called **tropisms**.

Positive phototropism – shoots bend towards the light.

Negative geotropism – shoots bend away from gravity.

Positive geotropism – roots bend with gravity.

Positive hydrotropism – roots bend towards moisture.

Other plant hormones control other plant activities like flowering and fruiting.

- Commercially, **giberellins** are sprayed on unpollinated flowers to make seedless fruits.
- **Rooting powder** contains hormones which stimulate cell division and therefore new roots on cuttings. Some are also used as weed killers on broad-leaved plants in lawns, for example, by disrupting their normal growth patterns.

Populations

A population is **how many** of one particular type of plant or animal there is in an **ecosystem**. The size of a population of each species depends on six main factors.

1. The total amount of food available.
2. Competition from members of the same and different species for food, space and a mate.
3. The number of predators or grazers that might eat the animal or plant in question.
4. Disease.
5. Death rate.
6. Immigration and emigration.

Pregnancy

Fertilisation of a human **egg** by a **sperm** can only occur in the top of an **oviduct** (fallopian tube). The cell called a **zygote** divides by **mitosis** as it travels down the oviduct to the **uterus** (womb) where it **implants** in the lining. The cells continue to multiply, some developing into the **embryo** and others into the **placenta**. The embryo develops organs rapidly over the first 12 weeks but is still tiny. Over the next 28 weeks it is called a **foetus** and grows enormously.

- The **amnion** is the **bag** that holds the foetus. It is full of **amniotic fluid** which **protects** the foetus from physical bumps.

- The placenta is where mother and baby's blood come close together for exchange of materials. Food and oxygen diffuse across from the mother's blood and waste products are taken away by it. Harmful things can also pass from the mother to the embryo, e.g. alcohol, bacteria, viruses, drugs and carbon monoxide from cigarette smoking. These can damage the growing embryo/foetus.

- The umbilical cord links the placenta to the baby.

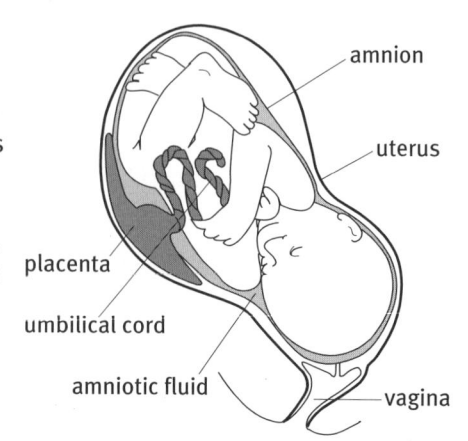

Producer

Producers are organisms which can make their own food. Most are green plants which can photosynthesise to make sugar. From this they can make oils and also proteins by adding nitrogen from nitrates. Producers provide food for all consumers.

See also Food chains and webs

Puberty

Humans have a long time as a child before they become sexually mature. At adolescence emotional and physical changes take place in response to hormones. These changes start earlier in females than in males. A brain hormone switches on the ovaries and testes.

- In females the ovaries make oestrogen which along with progesterone controls menstruation and secondary sexual characteristics, e.g. height spurt and breast development.
- In males the testes make sperm and testosterone which causes the secondary sexual characteristics, e.g. height spurt and voice breaking.

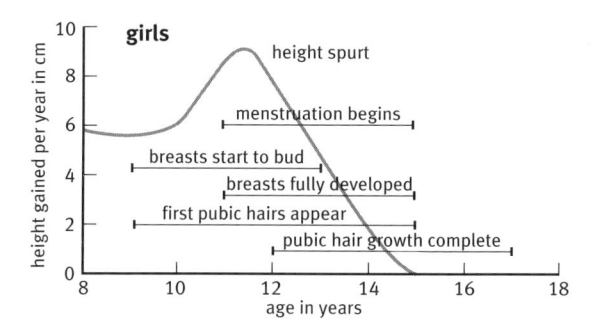

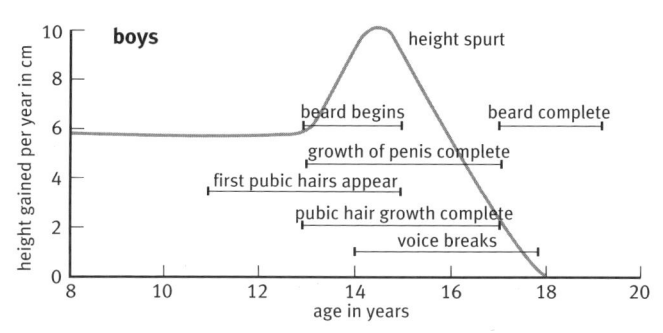

Pyramids of numbers and biomass (trophic levels)

When the numbers of organisms in a community are estimated it is usual to find more producers than consumers. The numbers at each feeding level (trophic level) can be represented by blocks in the form of a pyramid. Sometimes pyramids look wrong if the producer is very large, e.g. oak tree, or the consumers are very small, e.g. fleas.

Pyramids of numbers

tertiary consumers
secondary consumers
primary consumers
producers

numbers of individuals

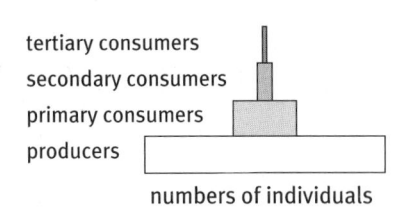

500 Fleas
1 Owl
5 Weasels
100 Woodmice
5000 Blackberries

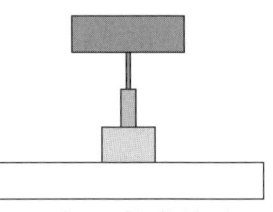

numbers of individuals

Pyramids of biomass

These use the mass of living organisms rather than simply the number. This more truly represents the feeding relationship. The pyramid is as above but the fleas' block is narrower than the owl's.

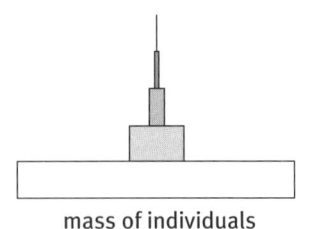

mass of individuals

Exam tip

You must know how to construct pyramids.

Reflexes

Reflexes are rapid automatic responses to stimuli. They protect living things from injury.

Stimulus → Receptor → Sensory neurone → CNS (Relay neurone) → Motor neurone → Effector → Response

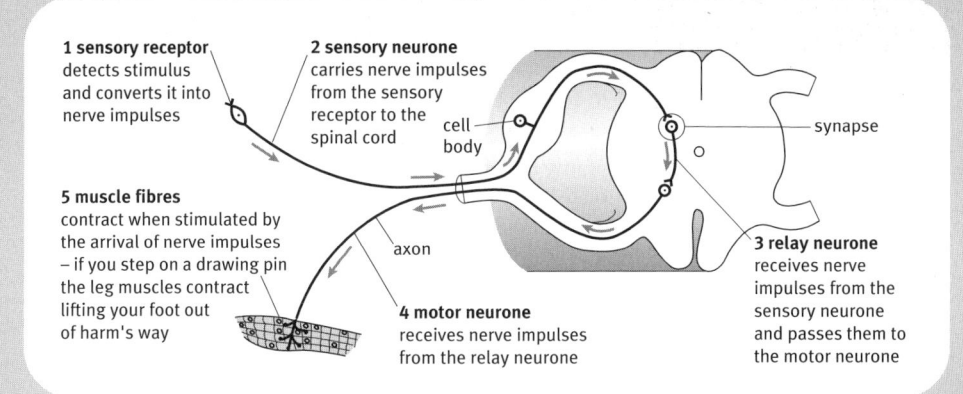

1 sensory receptor detects stimulus and converts it into nerve impulses

2 sensory neurone carries nerve impulses from the sensory receptor to the spinal cord

cell body

synapse

5 muscle fibres contract when stimulated by the arrival of nerve impulses – if you step on a drawing pin the leg muscles contract lifting your foot out of harm's way

axon

4 motor neurone receives nerve impulses from the relay neurone

3 relay neurone receives nerve impulses from the sensory neurone and passes them to the motor neurone

Reproductive systems

The female reproductive organs

- The lining of the **uterus** is where a fertilised egg can grow into a baby.
- The **oviduct** is a tube down which an egg travels to get to the uterus. The egg can only get fertilised high up in the tube.
- The **ovaries** produce eggs – one every month. They also produce the hormones which control the menstrual cycle.

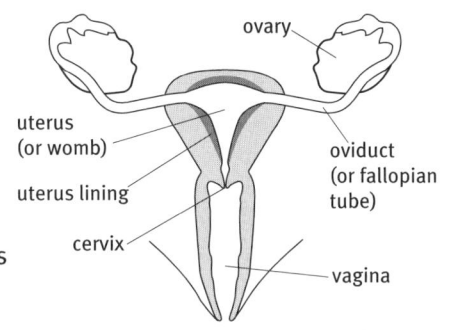

ovary
uterus (or womb)
oviduct (or fallopian tube)
uterus lining
cervix
vagina

The male reproductive organs

- **Sperm** are made in the **testes**.
- The **prostate gland** and seminal vesicle make a nutritious fluid for the sperm to swim in. This fluid is mixed with sperm as they pass by. The final mixture of sperm and fluid is called **semen**.
- During sexual intercourse the semen passes out of the body through an erect penis.

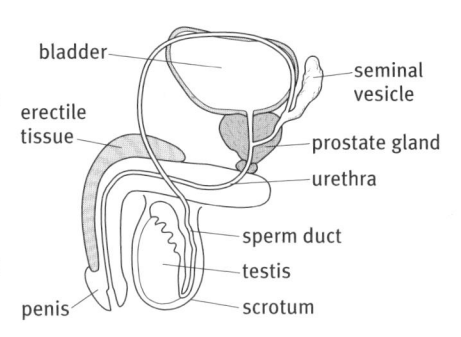

bladder
seminal vesicle
erectile tissue
prostate gland
urethra
sperm duct
testis
penis
scrotum

41

Respiration

- **Respiration** is the process in all living cells which releases **energy** from glucose to do **work**.
- **Aerobic respiration** needs plenty of **oxygen** and releases all the energy in the glucose.

Word equation

Glucose + Oxygen → Energy + Carbon Dioxide + Water

Chemical equation

$C_6H_{12}O_6 + 6O_2$ → Energy + $6CO_2 + 6H_2O$

- **Anaerobic respiration** can happen without oxygen, but very little energy is released.
- In humans it often happens during vigorous exercise when muscles can't get enough oxygen. Glucose is only partially broken down to **lactic acid**.

Word equation

Glucose → a little Energy + Lactic Acid

- The person is said to have built up an oxygen debt. Once the exercise has finished oxygen is rapidly returned to the muscles by an increase in heart and breathing rates. The lactic acid is then broken down completely to release more energy aerobically. A good measure of fitness is how quickly you can recover to normal pulse and breathing rates after doing some vigorous exercise. This is called the recovery time. Before the lactic acid is broken down it may cause cramp in the muscles, which is painful and may be dangerous when swimming.

In **yeast**, anaerobic respiration is called **fermentation**. The end-products are a little energy, alcohol and carbon dioxide.

Word equation

Glucose → a little Energy + Alcohol + Carbon Dioxide

We use the fact that alcohol is produced when we make wine and beer. In bread-making it's the carbon dioxide that makes the bread dough rise.

Exam tip

You must learn these equations. Practise writing them out. Compare aerobic respiration equations with photosynthesis – what do you notice?

Senses

Sense organs detect changes in the environment, i.e. stimuli. They contain **receptor cells** which produce electrical nerve impulses in response to a variety of **stimuli**.

- ear – sound and balance
- eye – light
- nose – chemicals (taste and smell)
- tongue – chemicals (bitter, salt, sour, sweet tastes)
- skin – touch, pressure and temperature change.

Selective breeding

Selective breeding is also called **artificial selection**. It involves humans choosing animals or plants with characteristics they think may be attractive or useful to us. They then breed from them. We select the offspring which match what we want and breed from them and so on.

This artificial selection has allowed us to produce many useful varieties, e.g.

- milking cows with disease resistance and high milk yields
- short-stemmed wheat with disease resistance, which puts more energy into making seeds.

Sex determination

- Humans have 46 chromosomes in their cell nuclei.
- One of the 23 pairs is made up of the sex chromosomes.
- Females have two identical X-chromosomes (XX).
- Males have one X-chromosome and one shorter Y-chromosome (XY).
- All egg cells have an X-chromosome, but half of all male sperm have an X-chromosome and half a Y-chromosome.
- The sex of a baby is determined by which sperm has fertilised the egg.

See also Fertilisation

Smoking (tobacco)

Smoking tobacco is a very serious cause of ill-health. There are over 350 different chemicals in cigarette smoke, many of which cause harm.

- The drug nicotine in cigarettes is addictive, making it difficult to give up smoking.
- Nicotine paralyses cilia in the windpipe which, along with clogging up by tar, allows the smoke contents to settle in the lungs. The only way to get rid of the tar, etc. is coughing.
- The chemicals in tar can cause lung cancer. Nine out of every ten lung cancer patients smoke.
- The surface of the **alveoli** in the lungs is **damaged** leading to diseases like **emphysema** and **bronchitis**. 20 000 people die each year in Britain of these conditions.
- **Carbon monoxide** in smoke causes narrowing of blood vessels. It leads to heart attacks, strokes and general poor circulation, which may lead to amputation of limbs. 100 000 people die of smoking-related heart disease each year in Britain.

Species

A species is a group of organisms which can interbreed and produce fertile offspring.

See also Biodiversity and population

Temperature control

The human body temperature has to be kept at 37°C to work properly. There is a **thermostat** in the hypothalamus of the brain called the **thermoregulatory centre**. It controls keeping heat in (conservation), heat loss and production of heat.

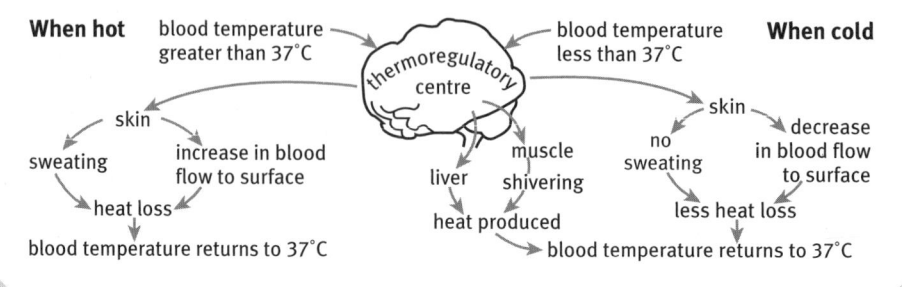

When hot
blood temperature greater than 37°C → thermoregulatory centre
- skin → sweating → heat loss
- increase in blood flow to surface → heat loss

blood temperature returns to 37°C

thermoregulatory centre → muscle, liver, shivering → heat produced

When cold
blood temperature less than 37°C
- skin → no sweating → less heat loss
- decrease in blood flow to surface → less heat loss

blood temperature returns to 37°C

Transpiration

Transpiration is the loss of water from the leaves of a plant.

- It is caused by evaporation of water from inside of leaves and diffusion of the water vapour through stomata into the air.
- It causes water to move up the xylem tubes from roots, through stems to leaves. This is called the **transpiration stream**. Minerals are also transported along with the water.
- Transpiration also **cools** the plant.

The **rate of transpiration** is affected by **environmental factors**.

- Hot, dry, windy and sunny conditions all increase transpiration.
- Cool, humid, still and dull conditions decrease transpiration.

Transport in plants (xylem and phloem)

Plants have a system of **tubes** or **vessels** in which to **transport** materials inside themselves. There are two separate sets of tubes called **xylem** and **phloem**. Xylem cells transport water. These cells have a substance called **lignin** in their cell walls. Lignin makes the cell walls **strong** and **waterproof**. The insides of the xylem cells break down and the cells become empty tubes. Xylem cells are found throughout the plant. Phloem cells contain living **cytoplasm**. They form a system of very **narrow tubes** which transport **sugars, amino acids**, etc. to all parts of the plant. They use up energy to do this.

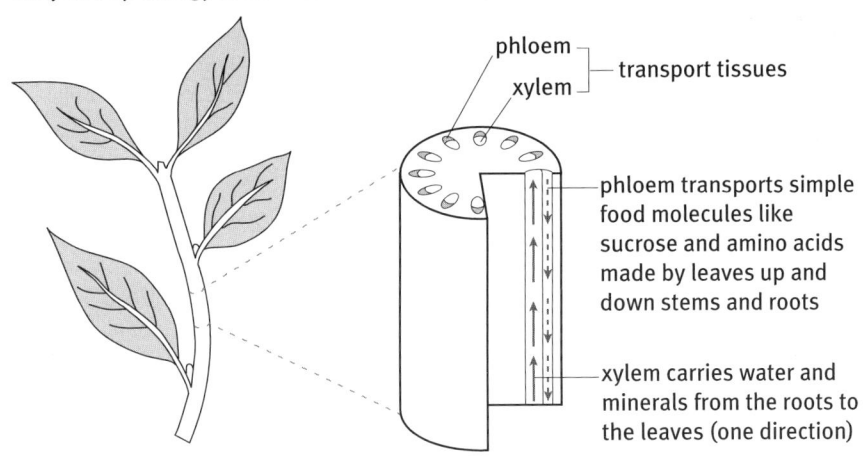

phloem
xylem — transport tissues

phloem transports simple food molecules like sucrose and amino acids made by leaves up and down stems and roots

xylem carries water and minerals from the roots to the leaves (one direction)

Variation

Variations in plants and animals are how members of the same species look or behave slightly differently from each other.

There are 2 main causes of variation.

1. Genetic variation caused by different genes/alleles.
2. Environmental variation caused by differences in the environment, e.g. amount of light or food, minerals, etc.

When both affect a feature the variation is said to be **continuous** e.g. height or weight. When a feature is either one thing or another, e.g. blue or brown eyes, it is said to be **discontinuous**.

Viruses

Viruses are not cells.

- They are very very small, 1/100th the size of a bacterium or 1/10000th the size of a human cell.
- They can only live **inside** the **cells** of other organisms and **always** cause harm.
- They consist of a **protein coat** with a **DNA** or **RNA** strand inside.
- They invade cells and then take them over in order to make more viruses.
- The cells then burst, releasing all the new viruses which can then invade more cells.
- They cause disease in plants, animals and bacteria.

Many human diseases are caused by viruses, e.g. colds, flu, chicken pox. The **HIV** (Human Immunodeficiency Virus) is a major problem world-wide as it leads to the disease **AIDS** (Acquired Immuno-Deficiency Syndrome) which is **fatal**. The only way a virus can be killed in a body is by the **immune system**. The problem for people with AIDS is that it is the immune system which the virus affects, so other diseases cannot be fought.

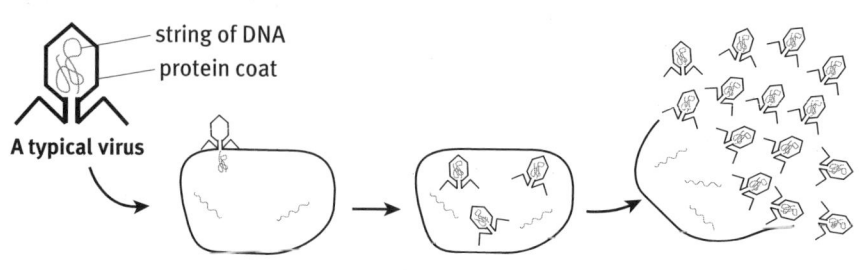